Reading Essentials in Science

GLOBAL ISSUES

Energy Sources

KAREN E. BLEDSOE

PERFECTION LEARNING®

Editorial Director: Susan C. Thies
Editor: Paula J. Reece
Design Director: Randy Messer
Book Design: Lori Gould, Emily J. Greazel
Cover Design: Michael A. Aspengren

A special thanks to the following for his scientific review of the book:
Wayne B. Merkley, Professor of Biology, Drake University

Image Credits:

© Yann Arthus-Bertrand/CORBIS: p. 17 (top); © Roger Ressmeyer/CORBIS: pp. 18 (bottom), 19, 23, 24; © Kennan Ward/CORBIS: p. 30 (bottom); © Charles O'Rear/CORBIS: p. 32 (bottom); © Reuters NewMedia Inc./CORBIS: p. 37; © Associated Press: p. 20

© Comstock Royalty-Free: p. 21; © Royalty-Free/CORBIS: front cover, pp. 1, 2–3, 6 (top), 9, 10 (girl blowing bubble), 15, 26, 27, 42 (background), 44–45; Clipart.com: pp. 8, 14; Corel Professional Photos: pp. 12, 22, 46–47, 48; LifeART © 2003 Lippincott, Williams, & Wilkins: p. 18 (top); NOAA: p. 11; Perfection Learning Corporation: pp. 5 (bottom), 13, 16, 17 (bottom), 25, 29 (bottom), 30 (top), 31, 32 (top), 34, 42 (chart), 43 (chart); PhotoDisc: p. 43 (background); Photos.com: back cover, pp. 5 (top), 6 (bottom), 7, 10 (tire, crayons, glasses), 18 (middle), 29 (top), 33, 38, 40, 41

Text © 2004 by Perfection Learning® Corporation.
All rights reserved. No part of this book may be reproduced, stored in a retrieval system, or transmitted in any form or by any means, electronic, mechanical, photocopying, recording, or otherwise, without prior permission of the publisher. Printed in the United States of America.

For information, contact
Perfection Learning® Corporation
1000 North Second Avenue, P.O. Box 500
Logan, Iowa 51546-0500.
Phone: 1-800-831-4190
Fax: 1-800-543-2745
perfectionlearning.com

1 2 3 4 5 6 PP 08 07 06 05 04 03
ISBN 0-7891-6076-5

Table of Contents

1. Energy Everywhere 4
2. Fossil Fuels as Energy 7
3. Nuclear Energy 14
4. Sun and Wind as Energy 21
5. Water and the Earth as Energy 28
6. Energy in the Future 33
7. Energy Conservation 38
   Internet Connections and Related Readings . . 44
   Glossary 46
   Index 48

Chapter One

Energy Everywhere

Think about all the forms of **energy** around you as you read this book. Electrical energy powers the electric lights overhead. Light energy reflects off the pages and into your eyes so you can see. Chemical energy sends signals from your eyes to your brain. More chemical energy powers the muscles in your arm so that you can turn the page. Then when you move your arm to turn the page, you are creating mechanical energy.

Perhaps you've heard about energy shortages. Yet all around you are many forms of energy. What is the problem?

What is energy?

Energy is difficult to define in a simple way. It isn't a substance. It isn't a feeling. The definition of energy is "the ability to do work." Think of it as something that makes things happen.

It is easy to misunderstand what energy is because we use the word *energy* in ways other than the scientific definition. For instance, when a friend says, "I have a lot of energy," your friend may mean she is feeling good that day. But energy isn't a feeling.

There are many forms of energy. Each form can be converted into another form. When you rub your hands together fast, your hands feel warm. You have converted mechanical energy into heat energy. When you light a candle, the chemical energy in the wax is converted into heat energy and light energy.

All forms of energy may be either potential or kinetic. Think of **potential energy** as stored energy. When you hold a ball in your hand, ready to drop it, the ball has potential energy.

Kinetic energy is energy associated with motion. When you release the ball, the potential energy is converted into kinetic energy as the ball falls.

When we talk about the energy we use every day to power our cars and heat our homes, we are often talking about various forms of potential energy. The gasoline that is put into a car's tank contains potential energy in the form of chemical energy. As it burns in the car's engine, it creates heat energy. Some of the energy is converted into mechanical energy, which makes the car's wheels turn. In this way, the potential energy in the gasoline is converted to the kinetic energy of the car's motion.

What is an energy crisis?

Sometimes there is a shortage of an energy source that we need to make our society run. Gasoline, diesel fuel, and other fuels are made from **crude oil**, oil that is naturally found underground. These forms of chemical energy are used to run cars, trucks, trains, airplanes, and many other forms of transportation. In the 1970s, the world experienced an oil shortage. The price of gasoline went up. This increased the cost of goods that had to be transported. People refer to this as an **energy crisis**. More recently, the West Coast of the United States had an electricity shortage. Prices for electricity went up. This was another energy crisis.

During the 1970s, the United States depended on foreign countries for much of its oil. In 1973, OPEC (The Organization of Petroleum Exporting Countries) refused to sell any more oil to the United States, causing an energy crisis. During this time, the price of gasoline rose from $.30 to $1.20 a gallon.

So far, most energy crises have been the result of the amount of energy that is sold. However, there is concern that certain forms of energy might soon be used up entirely. But are the forms of energy we commonly use all we have to choose from? Should we be working toward developing alternative forms of energy? In this book, you will read about many forms of energy and some of the benefits and drawbacks of each.

Chapter Two

Fossil Fuels as Energy

Nonrenewable energy sources come from resources that are limited, or can be used up. Oil and coal are considered nonrenewable resources. These resources were produced over the course of millions of years. That's why they are called *fossil fuels*. However, since only a certain amount of oil and coal exists worldwide, the supply can eventually run out if we continue using these fuels.

The origins of coal and oil

Coal is made from the remains of ancient swamps. When plants died, they fell into the water and sank to the bottom. Layer upon layer accumulated for thousands of years. The partly decayed plant matter changed into soft, dark **peat**. Over time, the peat was compressed and heated by the Earth, changing it into coal.

Crude oil comes from the remains of plants and animals on ancient sea floors. In the distant past, small organisms sank to the bottom of shallow seas. Over thousands of years, layers of sand and silt built up on top of the buried organisms. Heat from below the Earth's crust caused chemical and physical changes in the buried remains to produce crude oil.

How coal is mined

Coal from exposed seams in the Earth's crust was used as fuel in China and in the British Isles as early as 1100 B.C. People began mining coal in Europe during the Middle Ages, a period that lasted between the 5th and 15th centuries. At first, coal was carried out by hand in baskets or wheelbarrows. Sometimes mules, horses, or dogs were used to haul coal. More often, poor women and children did the hauling, while men dug the coal. Then early in the 19th century, steam engines supplied the power to move carts of coal along steel tracks.

Where is coal found?

Most coal is found in large deposits called *coal beds*. The coal beds are made up of seams, bands of coal separated by layers of clay, rock, or other mineral substances. Seams can be a fraction of an inch to several hundred feet thick.

Today, machines do much of the work in coal mines. Some coal mines are underground. In areas where the coal seams are near the surface and run horizontal to the surface, strip mining is a cheaper way to **extract** coal. In this method, earth-moving equipment removes the layer of dirt and rock that covers the coal seam. Once the coal is exposed, it is usually broken up by explosives. Then it is loaded into huge trucks that carry it to processing facilities.

How coal is used

Today, most coal is used to supply energy to electric companies. Power plants burn coal to run steam **turbines**, fanlike machines that generate electricity.

Coal hogs!
Electric utility companies use more than four-fifths of the coal mined in the United States.

Take some petroleum and call me in the morning.
People used to rub "tar water" on wounds and sores or ingest it for illnesses. They believed that because it smelled strong and tasted bad, it drove away disease. Today we know that this isn't true, but petroleum does have uses in modern medicine. It is used to make mineral oil, which is used as a laxative and skin softener, and petroleum jelly, which is used in ointments.

The history of petroleum

Crude oil, also known as *petroleum*, has been used for thousands of years. It was first collected after it would seep to the Earth's surface. Then it was used as tar on boats and road surfaces. Sometimes it was used as medicine. Occasionally, it was burned for light.

The gasoline engine was invented in the late 19th century. In the early 20th century, Henry Ford began making affordable cars. Airplanes and motorcycles were invented. Diesel trains replaced old steam engines. The world needed gasoline and diesel fuel for these new, faster forms of transportation. These fuels are produced from crude oil.

In 1908, oil was discovered in Persia, which today is called Iran. In 1938, oil was discovered in Saudi Arabia. In the United States, massive oil fields were found in Texas. The petroleum industry grew dramatically. Today, two-thirds of the world's oil comes from the Middle East.

How crude oil is extracted

Crude oil is extracted using steel drill bits attached to a drill pipe. Oil in a deposit is under high pressure. Have you ever seen a picture of oil gushing from the top of a well? In the early days of oil drilling, the oil gushed out as soon as the drill hit the deposit. However, modern equipment prevents this from happening. After the crude oil is removed from the ground, a pipeline, ship, or barge carries it to a **refinery**. There the crude oil is separated. This creates many useful products.

Petroleum products

Environmental issues

Oil spills are a major environmental problem associated with petroleum. When oil tankers leak, the crude oil can drift to beaches and rocky shores, where it kills wildlife. The largest oil spill in the United States occurred when the *Exxon Valdez* spilled into Prince William Sound, Alaska, in March 1989. The oil tanker dragged along the ground, and nearly 11 million gallons of crude oil spilled.

That's a lot of oil!

Although 11 million gallons of oil is considered a big spill, it is less than 2 percent of the amount of oil used daily in the United States!

How much is 11 million gallons?

It would be equal to the oil drained from 8.8 million cars. And it would fill up
- 3 1/2 school gyms,
- 44 high school swimming pools, or
- 92 average houses.

11

Oil refinery

Burning fossil fuels, such as coal and petroleum, also releases many pollutants. One pollutant, sulfur, causes acid rain. Another, carbon dioxide, may increase the **greenhouse effect**, causing the global temperature to rise. Sunlight causes a chemical reaction between petroleum **emissions** and nitrogen gas, creating **ozone**. While the ozone layer high in the atmosphere protects us from harmful ultraviolet radiation, ground-level ozone is a pollutant. Ozone near the ground can cause smog, a mixture of fog and smoke or other pollutants, which is harmful to plant life and makes breathing difficult for many people.

Are we running out?

Because petroleum is a limited resource, the world could run out. It's just that no one's sure when. During the oil crisis of the 1970s, people believed that the world would run out of petroleum by the 1990s.

However, the invention of more fuel-efficient cars reduced the amount of petroleum each car uses. Better extraction techniques and the discovery of new oil fields have increased oil production. These developments extended the lifespan of the world's oil supply.

The U.S. Department of Energy believes that oil will continue to be the main energy source throughout the world for at least 20 more years. Right now, oil provides 40 percent of the world's energy needs. **Renewable energy** sources, or sources that can't be used up, supply only about 5 percent. The U.S. Department of Energy expects this figure to rise to only 7–8 percent by 2020.

The bottom line is that no one knows for sure how long the world's oil supply will last. An increase in fuel efficiency would extend the supply. But as populations increase, so do the world's energy needs. One thing is certain—if the world continues using petroleum, eventually the supply *will* run out.

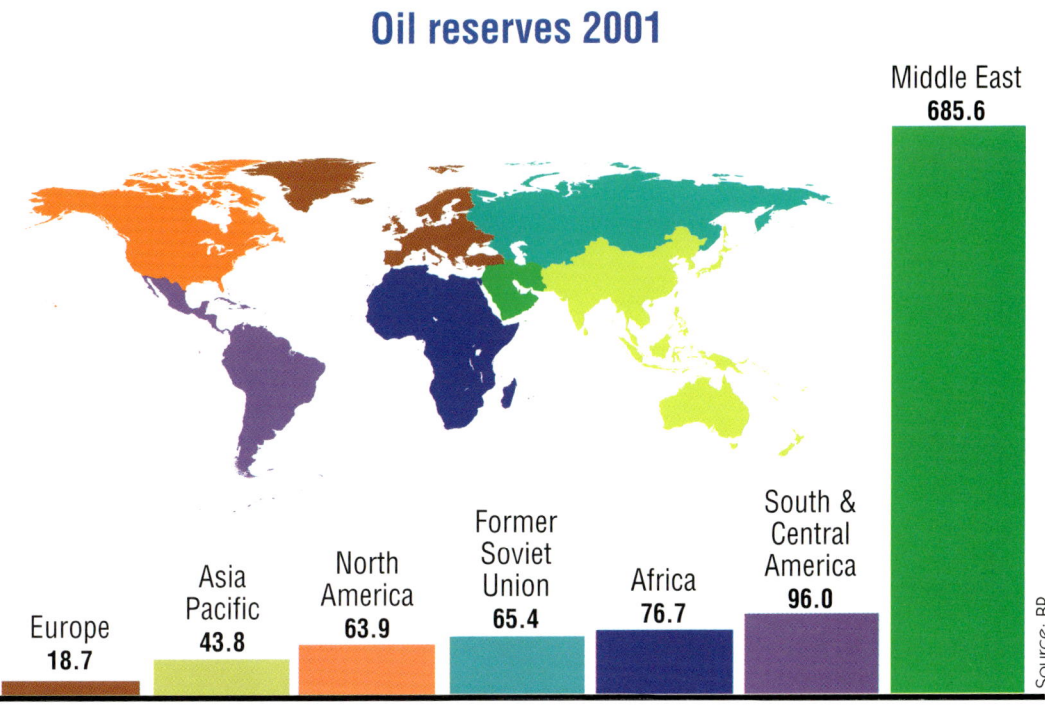

Chapter Three

Nuclear Energy

Nuclear power is also a nonrenewable energy source. However, it is an alternative to using fossil fuels for generating electricity. Since the 1950s, nuclear power plants have generated the electricity to light up homes and businesses. Nuclear reactors can create large amounts of electricity while producing little pollution. However, nuclear reactors can also produce big problems.

What is nuclear energy?

You don't have to be a nuclear scientist to understand the basics of nuclear energy. You just have to start with its simplest form. The tiny, basic unit of all substances is the **atom**. Nuclear energy is energy that is trapped inside each atom.

A true genius

Have you ever heard of the equation $E=mc^2$? This is the work of Albert Einstein, the world's most famous scientist. This equation basically explains that matter can be changed into energy. Scientists used this equation to figure out nuclear energy and to help create atomic bombs.

Nuclear power plant

Nuclear energy comes from an element called **uranium**. Uranium is naturally **radioactive**. That means that an atom of uranium can release a large amount of energy. As atoms of uranium split, they release energy in the form of heat. Splitting an atom is called *fission*.

After uranium is dug out of the ground, it is made into tiny pellets. These are placed into long rods that are put into a nuclear power plant's reactor. Inside the reactor, uranium atoms are split apart in a controlled **chain reaction**. Control rods regulate the fission in nuclear power plants to make sure it doesn't go too fast. The effect of an uncontrolled chain reaction could be an atomic explosion.

Where did uranium come from?

Uranium began to form a part of the Earth's crust after being released from an exploding star billions of years ago. Uranium is the heaviest natural element.

Fission can create large amounts of heat. In a nuclear power plant, the heat is used to boil water to run steam turbines. The turbines generate electricity.

15

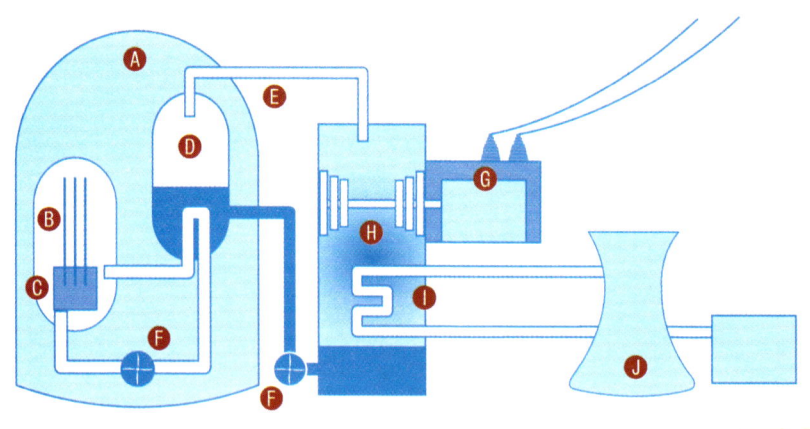

- **A** Containment structure
- **B** Control rods
- **C** Reactor
- **D** Steam generator
- **E** Steam line
- **F** Pump
- **G** Generator
- **H** Turbine
- **I** Cooling water condenser
- **J** Cooling tower

Activity

Simulating nuclear reactions

Control rods are used to make sure the nuclear reaction doesn't get out of control, causing an atomic explosion. Try this activity, which demonstrates nuclear reactions.

You'll need a set of dominoes; a ruler; and a flat, sturdy table.

On one section of the table, arrange part of the dominoes on end in the pattern shown below.

On another section of the table, arrange the remaining dominoes in two straight rows. Go back to the first pattern you arranged. Knock over the single domino in front. What happens? Go to the two straight rows of dominoes. Knock over the first domino in one of the lines. What happens?

Now take the ruler and hold it between any of the dominoes in the second line. Knock over the first domino. What happens now?

The first pattern of dominoes you created represents an uncontrolled nuclear chain reaction, such as an atomic explosion. The straight lines of dominoes represent what happens in a nuclear reactor. The ruler served as a control rod, regulating the chain reaction.

Towns near Chernobyl had to be abandoned.

Nuclear reactor accidents

Because nuclear reactors contain radioactive materials and can generate enough heat to cause fires and explosions, reactor operators have to pay close attention to safety. While there have been very few reactor accidents, a single accident can be disastrous.

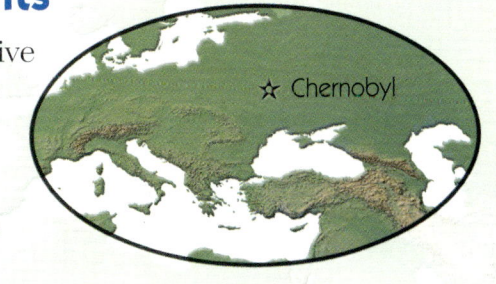

The world's worst nuclear reactor accident occurred at the Chernobyl nuclear power plant in the Ukraine, which was then part of the Soviet Union. On April 26, 1986, engineers were carrying out an experiment with one of the reactors when the cooling system turned itself off. As the engineers tried to fix the problem, they failed to notice a dangerous buildup in one area of the reactor. The nuclear reactor suddenly went out of control, shattering the fuel. The top of the reactor was blown off. Several chemical explosions followed, scattering fragments that caused local fires. Thirty-one people were killed immediately, and 500 more were hospitalized. Some died from radiation poisoning. Rates of thyroid cancer are still very high in the region.

What causes thyroid cancer—and what is the thyroid?

The thyroid is a gland located in the neck. It is responsible for controlling metabolism and growth. Metabolism refers to interactions that provide the energy and nutrients needed to stay alive. Thyroid cancer can be caused by exposure to radioactive iodine, an element that is absorbed by the thyroid. Almost 2000 cases of thyroid cancer have resulted from the Chernobyl disaster, and most of these were found in children. Fortunately, thyroid cancer is very treatable, so few have died from the disease.

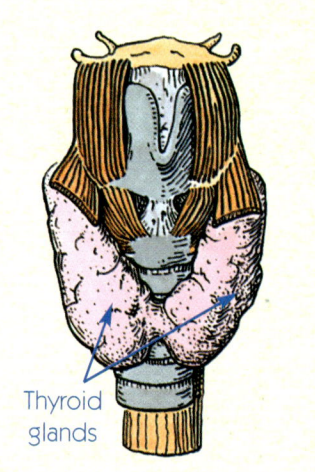

Thyroid glands

What happens to nuclear waste?

Nuclear reactions also make the waste product **plutonium**, which is extremely **toxic**, or poisonous. Safe storage of plutonium is a major problem. It must be stored safely for at least 10,000 years before most of the radioactivity decays. Designing a container to last that long is not easy. Not only is the engineering difficult, but language experts must design warning labels with symbols that can be understood by people 10,000 years from now.

Finding a safe site is also a problem. The site must be in a place that will not flood and where earthquakes are unlikely for the next 10,000 years. In 2002, the U.S. Senate approved a plan to build a nuclear waste storage facility deep inside Yucca Mountain in Nevada.

Yucca Mountain

Yucca Mountain has many of the qualities that a safe nuclear site needs. But many people in Nevada are not happy that their state has been chosen for storing nuclear waste. They are concerned about the safety of the site. Some people are worried that nuclear waste will be open to terrorist attacks while it is being transported.

In France, used nuclear fuel is recycled. The uranium and plutonium in the old fuel rods is recovered and processed into new fuel. This doubles the energy that the fuel produces and reduces the amount of radioactive waste produced. However, fuel recovery is expensive. It is cheaper to begin with fresh uranium. And some people are concerned that the recovered plutonium can be used in nuclear weapons.

A nuclear technician in France checks nuclear waste storage containers for radiation.

19

Why use nuclear energy?

With all the problems associated with nuclear reactors, why would anyone want to use them? In 1965, major cities throughout the United States experienced blackouts. The population was growing fast, and the usual sources could not supply enough electricity. People demanded increased energy production.

In 1971, President Richard Nixon decided that nuclear energy could help solve the nation's energy problems. The president's announcement helped increase research into nuclear power. By 1983, nuclear power was generating more electricity than natural gas, a fossil fuel. Only coal power plants produced more electricity.

Because the people of the world want inexpensive electricity, researchers everywhere are looking for ways to produce more electricity without using fossil fuels. Nuclear power is one alternative.

Tennessee Valley Authority's Watts Bar Nuclear Plant in Spring City, Tennessee

Chapter Four

Sun and Wind as Energy

Is there a safe way to produce energy without creating pollution and radioactive waste? Many people believe that renewable forms of energy are our best alternatives for the future. Renewable resources are those that will never run out, such as solar energy, wind power, hydropower, geothermal energy, and **biomass** energy.

Solar energy

The Earth receives two important things from the Sun every day—heat and light. Have you ever hung clothes outside to dry? That's a simple way that the Sun can be used to do work—in this case, dry your clothes. The Sun can be used to meet energy needs in other ways as well.

A million planets the size of Earth would fit inside the Sun. For energy to travel from the center of the Sun to the surface of the Sun takes millions of years. But from there, it only takes eight minutes for it to travel 93 million miles to Earth.

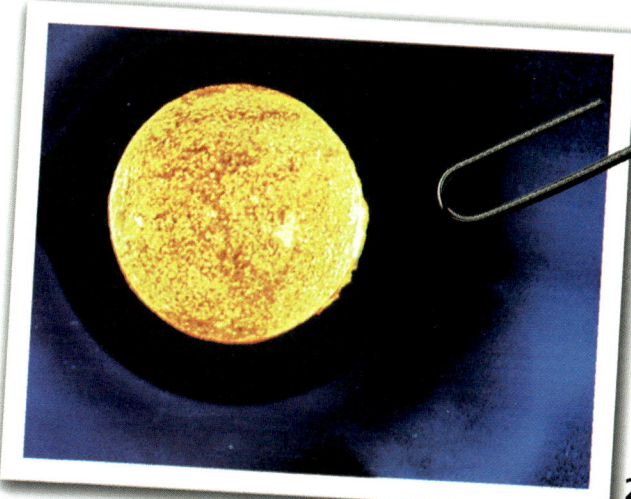

Solar heating

One way the Sun can be used for heating is through passive solar design. Buildings can be designed to make the most of **solar energy**. Passive solar designs have been used for centuries to keep homes warm or cool. The Incan city of Machu Picchu used solar heating. The houses had thick rock walls on the east side, which absorbed the Sun's heat in the morning. The rock then radiated heat all afternoon and evening. The city itself was built on the east side of a hill. The west-facing walls were backed with dirt, providing insulation. Some of today's passive solar heating systems rely on insulated glass, or glass designed to reduce the passage of heat. Homes may be built with large glass windows or attached greenhouses on the south side, which receives the most direct sunlight.

Powerful rays

The sunlight that shines on the United States in one day contains more than twice the energy the United States uses in an entire year!

Machu Picchu

22

Activity

Comparing the Sun's heat

Find out how much the Sun can heat things up in your house. Pick a sunny day to do this. You'll need at least one window on the south side and one on the north side of your home.

You'll need two dark cups that are the same size. You'll also need two pieces of dark-colored cardboard. (You can color them with a crayon or marker.)

Start your experiment in the morning. Fill both cups with water. Place one by a window on the south side of your house and one by a window on the north side. (Make sure the shades are up!) Cover each cup with one piece of cardboard, dark side up. Leave the cardboard on the cups all day.

When the Sun starts to set, collect both cups of water. Feel the water in each cup. Which is warmer? The water on the south side of your house should be warmer since it was heated more by the Sun.

Active solar energy uses solar panels to create heat or electricity. To use the Sun to heat water or a building, solar panels are installed on a building's roof. The Sun heats a liquid that passes through the panel. That liquid helps provide hot water or central heating for the building. This is not a new technology. In fact, from the 1920s until just before World War II, all residents of Florida heated their water with solar water heaters.

Solar panels on the roof heat this home.

Solar energy panels stand in rows in the Mojave Desert.

Solar electricity

Using solar panels to create electricity is fairly new, however. In fact, only a handful of solar thermal power plants exist worldwide. One is located in California's Mojave Desert. Built in 1984, it was the first commercial solar thermal power plant. It uses huge rows of solar mirrors to create electricity for more than 350,000 homes.

Electricity can also be directly converted from the Sun using its light instead of its heat. This is called *photovoltaics*. Photovoltaic systems convert light energy into electricity using solar cells. In the late 1950s, solar cells began being

What kind of word is *photovoltaics*?

Photo comes from the Greek word *phos*, which means "light." Sun . . . light . . . Makes sense so far, right? Voltaic is named for Alessandro Volta (1745–1827). Why? He was a pioneer in the study of electricity. We get the term *volt* from him, referring to a unit of electrical force. So *photovoltaics* means "light electricity." See, that wasn't such a hard word after all!

used to power U.S. space satellites. Today, simple solar cells power calculators and watches. More complicated systems generate electricity in water plants, homes, and even space stations.

Drawbacks of solar power

Solar power systems of any kind tend to be expensive. Few people can afford to have them installed in their homes, though the systems can pay for themselves in energy savings over time. Not all homes can use solar systems effectively either. People who live in areas with lots of rainy or overcast days may encounter difficulties.

Wind power

Just as the Sun can be used to produce energy, so can wind. And just as we could never use up the Sun, we will never run out of wind.

How wind makes electricity

Windmills may have been built in China as early as 200 B.C. The Dutch later built windmills to turn millstones for grinding grain. In the American West, windmills were used to pump water from deep wells.

Today's sleek windmills are electric generators called **wind turbines**. The spinning blades "catch" the wind. This changes the wind's direction from horizontal to vertical, causing the blades to spin. The blades then turn generators, creating power without producing pollution. Wind turbine blades are up to 50 feet long. The turbines can be as tall as ten stories.

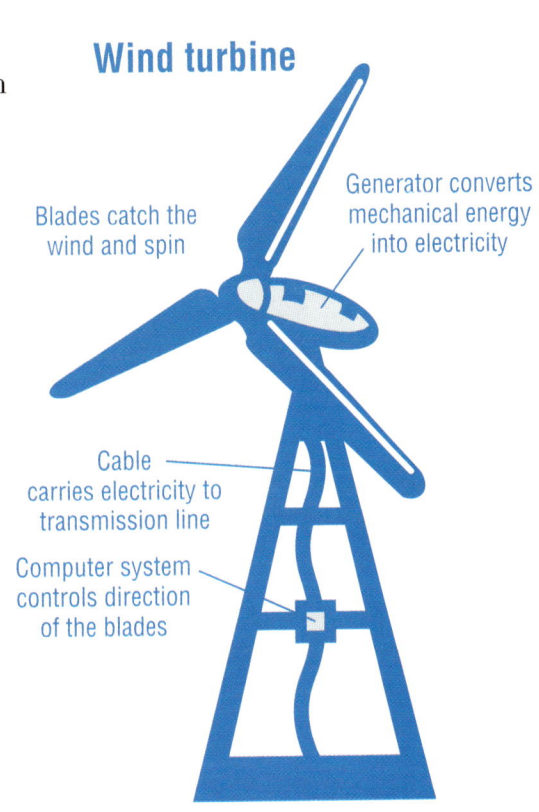

Wind turbine

Blades catch the wind and spin

Generator converts mechanical energy into electricity

Cable carries electricity to transmission line

Computer system controls direction of the blades

25

Where, oh where, are the wind farms?

There are 126 wind farms operating in the United States. California houses 88 of these, and Minnesota has 10.

Where wind power is being used today

The United States has enough wind turbines now to supply up to 4300 megawatts, about 1 percent of the country's electricity needs. Wind turbines in the Columbia Gorge, overlooking the Columbia River, will soon supply electricity to 70,000 homes in Oregon and Washington. Wind farms, large groups of turbines, are springing up throughout the Great Plains states, where cattle graze under turning blades.

Other countries have invested even more in **wind power**. Denmark has over 2000 wind turbines in place. Many households in Denmark belong to energy cooperatives. Between 100 and 200 people may form a cooperative. Members pool their money and buy a wind turbine together. One turbine can supply all the electricity needed for 50 to 100 homes. Or combined with other sources of electricity, the turbine can provide power for about 200 homes. Right now, wind power supplies about 18 percent of Denmark's electricity.

Drawbacks of wind power

Like all energy sources, wind power has its problems. The biggest problem is finding a place for the turbines where there is enough wind. Without wind, the turbines cannot produce power. Most turbines require wind speeds of at least 12 miles per hour to work efficiently. Large turbines need winds of at least 18 miles per hour.

Some wind-power companies are using ocean winds and building offshore wind turbines. The Cape Cod Wind Association plans to build a wind farm five miles off the coast of Massachusetts. The Association believes that the wind farm would be far enough offshore that it would not be visible, so people couldn't complain of its appearance. But many people in the area are against the plan. Air-traffic controllers worry that the turbines, which are all taller than the Statue of Liberty, could cause airplane accidents. Boaters complain that the turbines could interfere with boat navigation. The fishing industry is afraid that the wind turbines may harm migratory fish and other marine life.

Land-based wind turbines can also be hazardous to birds. A study by the California State Energy Commission in the early 1990s showed that during a two-year period, 500 birds of prey were killed in the area where 7000 wind turbines were operating near San Francisco. Since that time, engineers have been working on redesigning the turbines to reduce hazards to birds.

The biggest obstacle to developing wind power is the cost. Currently, wind-generated electricity costs about four times as much per kilowatt as electricity from coal-burning power plants. Governments often must offer rewards to companies to get them interested in developing wind power. Customers also want to get the best price and don't want to pay extra for wind power.

Chapter Five

Water and the Earth as Energy

How can using water or heat from the Earth be better than using fossil fuels as energy? Like solar power and wind power, water and heat from the Earth are renewable. Lakes, rivers, and oceans are replenished when it rains or snows, and the **core** of the Earth is continuously producing heat.

Hydropower

How water turns into electricity

Hydropower is the most often used renewable energy source for producing electricity. Hydropower is created by directing or channeling moving water. The amount of energy available depends on how fast the water is moving or how far it falls. For example, the Columbia River, between Washington and Oregon, moves very quickly and can produce a lot of electricity. Niagara Falls in New York also generates a lot of electricity because the water falls from a high point.

How much electricity do we get from hydropower?

In 2000, 7 percent of electricity generated in the United States was from hydropower. It accounted for 76 percent of renewable electricity production.

Today's turbines are so efficient that 90 percent of the kinetic energy in falling water is converted into electricity. As stored water from a reservoir behind a dam falls on the blades of the turbine, the turbine rotates. When the turbine rotates, it turns the generator, creating electrical energy.

The Grand Coulee Dam is the largest concrete dam in North America. Construction of the dam began in 1933, and the dam is considered one of the modern engineering wonders of the world.

Who produces hydropower?

The biggest producer of hydroelectric power in the United States is the Grand Coulee Dam on the Columbia River in Washington. The dam was completed in 1942. Currently, it is the third-highest producer of hydropower in the world. The top producer is in Turukhansk, Russia.

Drawbacks of hydropower

Hydropower is praised for being almost free and creating no waste or pollutants in the air. It isn't completely problem-free, however. Lakes do not constantly refresh themselves as rivers do. Any pollutants from industry and agriculture tend to remain in the lake behind the dam. Silt washed downstream can build up behind the dam. When the Aswan Dam was built on the Nile River in Egypt, farming practices along the river changed. For centuries, farmers had relied on annual floods, which covered their fields with fresh, nutrient-rich sediments. Now those sediments accumulate behind the dams, unable to make it to the fields.

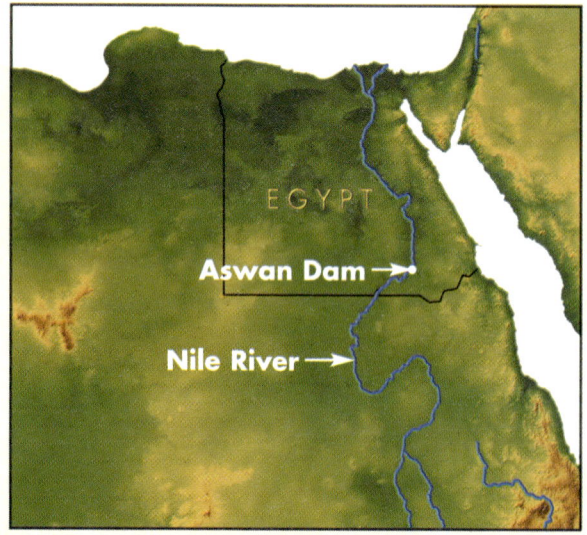

Dams can also harm migrating fish. Salmon swim downstream to the ocean when they are small. They spend several years in the ocean as they grow to adults. Then they migrate back upstream to spawn, or reproduce, and die. Dams can make it difficult for salmon to migrate. Young salmon swimming downstream can get swept into the turbines and killed. Mature salmon swimming upstream cannot jump over dams to get to the spawning grounds. Dams in areas where salmon migrate have built-in "fish ladders." These ladders look like staircases. Fish swim up the ladder by jumping from step to step.

This fish ladder enables fish to climb upstream from Pyramid Lake in Nevada.

Hydroelectric dams can have a cultural impact too. The reservoirs behind dams in Egypt flooded ancient Egyptian ruins. The reservoir behind Bonneville Dam on the Columbia River flooded Memaloose Island, which was a burial ground and sacred place for Native Americans in the region.

Geothermal energy

Just as water can produce renewable energy, so can the Earth. The Earth is made up of layers, similar to a boiled egg. Picture a boiled egg that has been cut in half. The yellow yolk in the center of the egg is like the core of the Earth, which is around 4000 miles deep. Temperatures there may reach over 9000°F! The soft egg white is like the **mantle** of the Earth. The mantle also contains layers. The top layer is made up of hot, liquid rock called *magma*. The **crust** of the Earth, similar to the thin eggshell, floats on the magma.

Lava on the loose

Sometimes magma breaks through the surface of the Earth in a volcano. It is then called *lava*.

Geothermal energy is heat energy produced in the Earth's hot, liquid interior. The energy can be used either directly as heat or indirectly to produce power.

Geothermal heat

Where magma comes close to the surface, it may heat groundwater. If that water comes up out of the ground, it creates a hot spring, which can be used for bathing or heating. The city of Bath, England, began as an ancient Roman colony built up around hot mineral springs. In the 18th century, Bath became a fashionable spa where people came to bathe in the hot waters and to drink the water. They believed the strong-tasting, mineral-rich waters could cure diseases.

Today, heat can be pulled from under the ground to heat houses and buildings. Water from hot springs is sometimes used to heat houses. Pipes containing hot water radiate heat into homes. In Iceland, nearly 80 percent of all homes are heated this way.

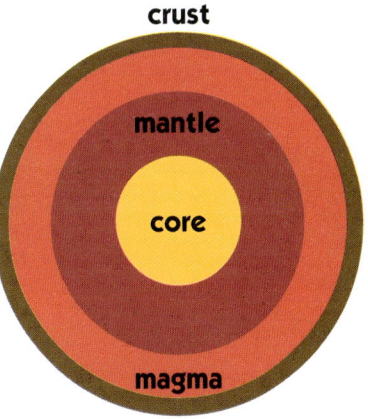

Geothermal electricity

A geothermal power plant is like a regular power plant except no fuels are burned to heat water to turn the steam turbines. Instead, production wells are drilled into **geothermal reservoirs**. The steam, heat, or hot water from the geothermal reservoirs travels up the wells to the Earth's surface, forcing turbine generators to spin, producing electricity. The used geothermal water is injected back into the reservoirs to be reheated.

How many geothermal plants are we talking about?

In 1999, there were 204 geothermal power plants in the United States, most of them located in California and Nevada.

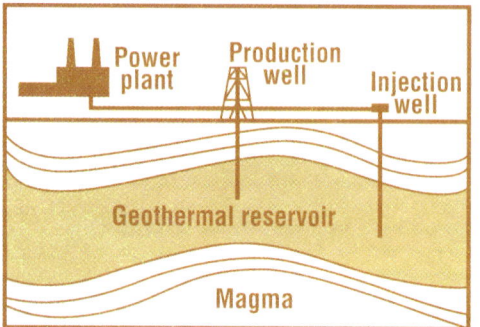

Drawbacks of geothermal energy

Some companies are exploring Yellowstone National Park in Wyoming. They are thinking about using the area for geothermal power. Many people are concerned that tapping into hot groundwater may affect the geyser system in Yellowstone.

Geothermal development can have cultural impacts also.

The geothermal facility at The Geysers in northern California is the world's largest source of geothermal power.

Some native Hawaiians objected to the development of geothermal plants on Hawaii. They believed that using volcanic heat to generate electricity was disrespectful toward the volcano goddess Pele.

Chapter Six

Energy in the Future

Humans will always need energy sources. If we continue using up fossil fuels at the present rate, the world will one day run out. Engineers and scientists, however, are constantly researching new sources of energy. Some promising new energy ideas are already on the market.

Energy from biomass

What is biomass?

Do you have a wood-burning fireplace? If you do, then you are using an alternative source of energy called *biomass*. Biomass is energy from wood, animal waste, and agricultural crops and waste. Along with logs, other wood products that can be used are sawdust, pruned tree branches, paper trash, and scraps from mills. Fast-growing trees, such as poplars and willows, and grasses like switchgrass and prairie bluestem can also be used to create biomass energy. Animal manure, along with crops such as sugarcane, corn, sugar beets, and grains, is also used.

Poplar trees

33

Biomass has been used for cooking and heating for thousands of years. In 1850, 91 percent of the energy used in the United States was biomass energy in the form of wood. Even today, biomass is still a main form of energy used by people in less developed countries.

How much biomass energy do we use today?

Biomass currently provides nearly 15 percent of the world's energy supply and 4 percent of that of the United States.

How biomass energy is produced

Biomass energy can be used to produce heat, electricity, or liquid fuels for motor vehicles. The main way of getting energy from biomass is by burning it. The heat created from burning the materials can be used for space heating or water heating. By using a steam turbine, electricity can be generated. Another way of creating energy is by fermenting the biomass to create liquid fuels. This means that the biomass is broken down into simpler substances. The most common example of this is the creation of ethanol by fermenting corn or sugarcane.

Ethanol is used mainly as a fuel for cars. It is usually blended with gasoline to make a product that is sometimes called *gasohol*. This gasoline-ethanol mixture burns hotter than plain gasoline. Pure ethanol burns too hot for today's engines. Engines must be redesigned to accept ethanol alone. Using ethanol in gasoline means we don't burn quite as much fossil fuel in our cars.

① Crops like corn are finely ground

② and separated into their component sugars.

③ The sugars are distilled to make ethanol,

④ which can be used as an alternative fuel,

⑤ which releases carbon dioxide that is reabsorbed by the original crops.

CO_2

Benefits and drawbacks of biomass energy

What are the benefits of using biomass energy? Burning biomass is better for the environment than burning fossil fuels. When fossil fuels are burned, carbon dioxide is released into the atmosphere, which contributes to global warming. When biomass is burned, carbon dioxide is also released. The difference is that biomass needs carbon dioxide to grow too. So biomass also takes in carbon dioxide. Some scientists even claim that biomass takes in more carbon dioxide than it releases. This means that biomass energy would not contribute to global warming, and it might even help slow it down.

Biomass crops can be planted where other crops cannot, and many do not have to be planted again every year. The plants could also help the environment by reducing soil erosion and water pollution. They can also provide habitat, or food and shelter, for a wide variety of wildlife. And using agricultural waste will also save it from piling on landfills.

Using biomass as an energy source in the United States means less oil imported from overseas. This helps keep the prices down in the United States. It also keeps as much as $25 billion in the United States that is normally sent overseas.

So far, it has been cheaper to use fossil fuels than biomass for energy. However, if fossil fuels start to run out, the prices will rise. People may also begin putting more importance on environmental benefits instead of cost in the future.

Energy from hydrogen

Hydrogen gas burns with explosive power. When it burns, the only waste product is water. It is a clean-burning fuel, which leads some scientists to believe that hydrogen could be the answer to the world's energy problems.

Benefits and drawbacks of energy from hydrogen

Hydrogen fuel cells are a promising result of a new line of research. These are devices similar to batteries that produce electricity using hydrogen. Hydrogen is very abundant in the universe, but it is only found in combination with other elements. So to use hydrogen, scientists must first separate it from those other elements.

Burning hydrogen as a fuel is exciting because it doesn't damage the environment. Hydrogen fuel cells produce a lot of electricity with no toxic waste. They are powerful enough to run cars or to heat and light homes and offices. They were used on board Apollo mission spacecraft and are used today on space shuttles to produce electricity and provide drinking water. So why aren't they used everywhere?

Hydrogen fuel cells have two big problems. The first is their cost. Fuel cells are expensive to produce. While a single fuel cell could provide the average home with more than enough electricity, few people can afford to buy one.

The second problem is it takes energy to produce hydrogen. The cheapest way to make pure hydrogen is to extract it from methane gas. However, the extraction process also produces carbon dioxide, which is a greenhouse gas. Plus, the most abundant source of methane is natural gas, which is another fossil fuel.

Water is another source of hydrogen. Water can be broken down into oxygen and hydrogen using electricity. However, it takes a lot of electrical energy to break down water. That electricity is most often produced by burning fossil fuels. If a cheaper way of breaking down water can be developed, hydrogen fuel cells could be made practical.

Hybrid engines

A practical way of producing hydrogen-fueled cars is still many years away. However, another alternative to the gasoline-powered car is already on the car lots—the hybrid-engine car.

In a standard car, gasoline fuels the engine, which supplies power to turn the transmission, which turns the wheels. Electricity can also turn the transmission, but today's electric cars are not practical. Electric cars usually go

Cars of the future

Engineers at General Motors, a major automobile manufacturer, are designing new cars that use hydrogen fuel cells. Because the cells are small, engineers do not have to design cars around a bulky engine. The latest ideas include a car chassis, the frame and wheels, that looks something like a skateboard. The parts that are normally underneath the hood are instead underneath the car, allowing for a roomier interior. One thing no one has designed yet is a hydrogen filling station for hydrogen-powered cars. Engineers will have to figure out how customers or station attendants can put hydrogen into the cars quickly and safely. They will also have to figure out how to transport hydrogen to these filling stations.

only 50 to 100 miles before they need a recharge. Gasoline-powered cars can go 300 miles or more between fill-ups. Filling a car with gasoline takes only a few minutes, while recharging an electric car can take hours.

Hybrid engine cars use both gasoline and electricity. They are highly fuel-efficient. They can get 60 miles to the gallon during city driving and 70 miles per gallon or more on the highway. This uses about half as much fuel as the most efficient gasoline-fueled cars.

Nissan Motors' first gasoline/electric hybrid car, the Tino Hybrid

Hybrid cars can also recover energy that is usually wasted while driving. A car may be capable of 200 horsepower, but drivers only use that much power when they "floor it." Most of the time, they only need 20 horsepower. This makes for an inefficient car. Hybrid cars can save energy by shutting off the engine when the car doesn't need it, such as when the car is stopped at a red light. The loss of kinetic energy when slowing down can also be recovered and stored in the battery. Toyota plans to eliminate gasoline-only cars from their line and produce only gas-electric hybrid cars by 2012.

Activity

Evaluating the state of your community

What futuristic energy technology can you buy in your area? Take an inventory of your community. You may find hybrid cars for sale on car lots. You may see ethanol being advertised at gas stations. Contact your local power company or visit its Web site to see if it is using any alternative forms of energy for generating electricity. Write a "state of the community" report to explain your findings.

Chapter Seven

Energy Conservation

Scientists and engineers around the world are working to find new sources of energy and develop practical uses for them. There are things you can do to be part of the solution to energy problems too. Though there are many alternative sources of energy being developed, most of our energy comes from fossil fuels. Conservation can help make the supply of fossil fuels last longer.

Being energy-efficient

Lighting

As you look around your home, you can probably find many ways you can use less energy. As you read this book, what kind of light are you using—fluorescent lamps or ordinary incandescent lightbulbs? Incandescent bulbs put out a lot of light but waste a lot of energy as heat. Fluorescent lights are filled with a gas, often mercury, under very low pressure. Electricity makes the gas glow. Once these lights are lit, they require very little electricity to keep on

Fluorescent lightbulb

glowing. Fluorescent bulbs are more expensive than incandescent bulbs, but they can last up to ten times longer, and they use one-fourth of the electricity. They are most practical in areas where people leave the lights on for 30 minutes or more, such as in living rooms.

> ### It keeps going . . . and going . . . and going . . .
>
> A lightbulb in the Livermore-Pleasanton Fire Department's Station Number Six in California has been burning continuously since 1901! This handblown bulb that glows with the use of carbon is the longest-burning bulb in the world. If left burning, regular incandescent bulbs would last between 750 and 2000 hours. Fluorescent bulbs can last 20,000 hours. As of June 8, 2002, this bulb had been burning more than 800,000 hours! You can see a "live" picture of the lightbulb 24 hours a day by going to its Web site, www.centennialbulb.org/.

Simply turning off lights when no one is in the room is a sure way to save energy. If there is a light in your home that everyone forgets to turn off, try making a sticker or sign to hang next to the switch as a reminder.

Appliances

Appliances also use a lot of electricity. They make up about 20 percent of a household's energy consumption. Newer appliances are designed to be as energy-efficient as possible. Many people find that when they buy new refrigerators or stoves, their electric bill drops. Their new appliances use less electricity than their old ones.

Do you help with laundry? If you do, what temperature do you use? About 80 percent of the energy used for washing clothes is in heating the water. Just washing clothes in warm water instead of hot can cut a load's energy use in half. Washing a full load instead of a small load will save more energy.

Would you rather load dishes into a dishwasher than wash them by hand? If so, you're in luck. Running a dishwasher uses 37 percent less water than washing the same load of dishes by hand. Turning off the heated dry setting and letting dishes air dry also saves energy. Conserving water means conserving energy. The biggest use of electricity in most cities is supplying water and cleaning it up after it's been used.

Heating and cooling

Heating and cooling a home uses lots of energy since most homes still use fossil fuels to regulate the temperature. One easy way to save energy is by turning down your thermostat in the winter

Thermostat

and up in the summer. Even a couple of degrees can save energy—and money. Programmable thermostats allow a person to adjust the thermostat automatically at night or when no one's home. Ceiling fans can also help heat or cool a house without using as much energy.

Do your windows have curtains? Shutting the curtains at night during the winter helps hold in the heat. You can also close the curtains during the day and open them at night in the summer to help keep the house cool.

Activity

Learning about insulation

Try this activity to see how insulation in your home helps keep it warm or cool. You will need two ice cubes that are the same size, three paper towels, and two small bowls.

First, put one of the ice cubes by the edge of one of the paper towels. Roll up the ice cube in the paper towel, and then wrap the edges of the towel around it. Wrap that same wrapped ice cube in the second and then the third paper towels.

Next, put the wrapped cube in one bowl and the unwrapped cube in the other. Let the bowls sit for an hour and then check back.

What does the plain ice cube look like? Is it melted or almost melted? Now unwrap the paper towels. How much of the ice cube is left? Which stayed cooler—the plain ice cube or the one wrapped up?

Each bowl represents a house. The ice cubes represent cool air in the summer and warm air in the winter. The paper towels are insulation. Without insulation, more of the cool or warm air escapes from the house (the ice cube melts). Less escapes when insulation is used.

Being a concerned consumer

Another way you can help reduce energy problems is by thinking when you shop. Think about all the products you or your family consumes. How much thought do you put into your purchases?

Buy locally

One way to help conserve energy is to buy products that are grown or made locally. For example, fruits and vegetables that are grown across the country or overseas require lots of fuel, usually fossil fuels, to get to your grocery store. Think about attending farmer's markets or buying products that you know didn't have far to travel.

Opt for reusable products

Farmer's market

Buying things that can be used again instead of disposable items will help save energy—the energy required to produce and transport those products. An example of a reusable product you can buy is batteries. If you own a battery-operated electronic device, such as a personal stereo or a handheld game, you know how quickly the batteries can run down. Many people already buy rechargeable batteries to save money.

Batteries can also be designed with different chemicals inside. A new silver polymer battery is being used by stock traders on the floor of the Chicago Mercantile Exchange and will soon be used on the New York Stock Exchange. Traders use handheld wireless devices for trading stocks all day long. The handheld devices had used lithium batteries, which hold a charge for only a few hours. The silver polymer batteries hold a charge all day and are more energy-efficient. The same technology can be used to make batteries for laptop computers.

Another way to reuse products is by taking your own bags with you when you go grocery shopping. Plastic bags are made from either oil or natural gas, both nonrenewable resources. They also add a lot of pollution, since most people use them once and then throw them away. Paper bags are made from trees, but only about 700 paper bags can be made from one 15-year-old tree. Think of how many paper bags a supermarket goes through in a day! If you do get disposable bags from the grocery store, think of ways to reuse them and then recycle them.

Recycle

Do you know if you have a recycling program in your community? Does your family participate in it? If you're unsure if a program exists, contact your city government to find out. Many items, including plastics, newspapers, white paper, cardboard, and aluminum cans, can easily be recycled. Recycling reduces the amount of energy required to make new products "from scratch." Along with recycling your trash, you can buy recycled products. This also helps cut down on the use of nonrenewable energy, such as fossil fuels.

Recycling saves energy— and trees!

What's an easy way to save one tree? Recycle 4 feet of paper. If every American recycled his or her newspaper just one day a week, it would save about 36 million trees a year! Making recycled newspaper takes only half as much energy as making fresh newsprint from trees.

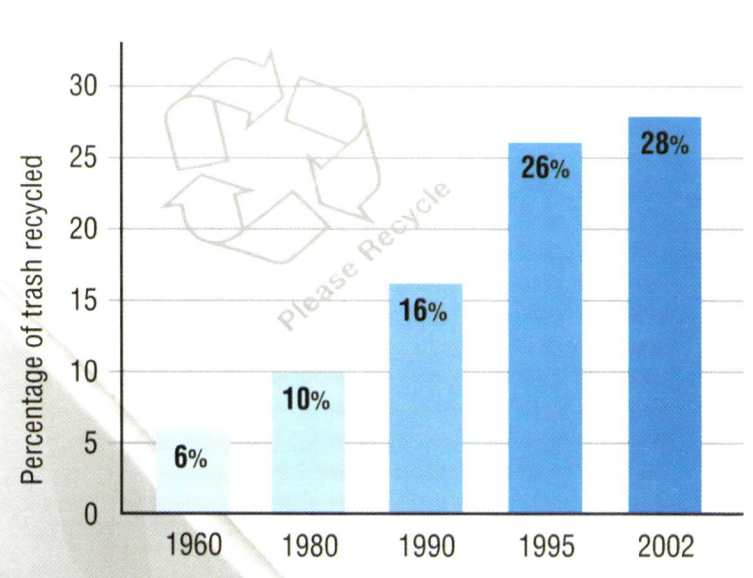

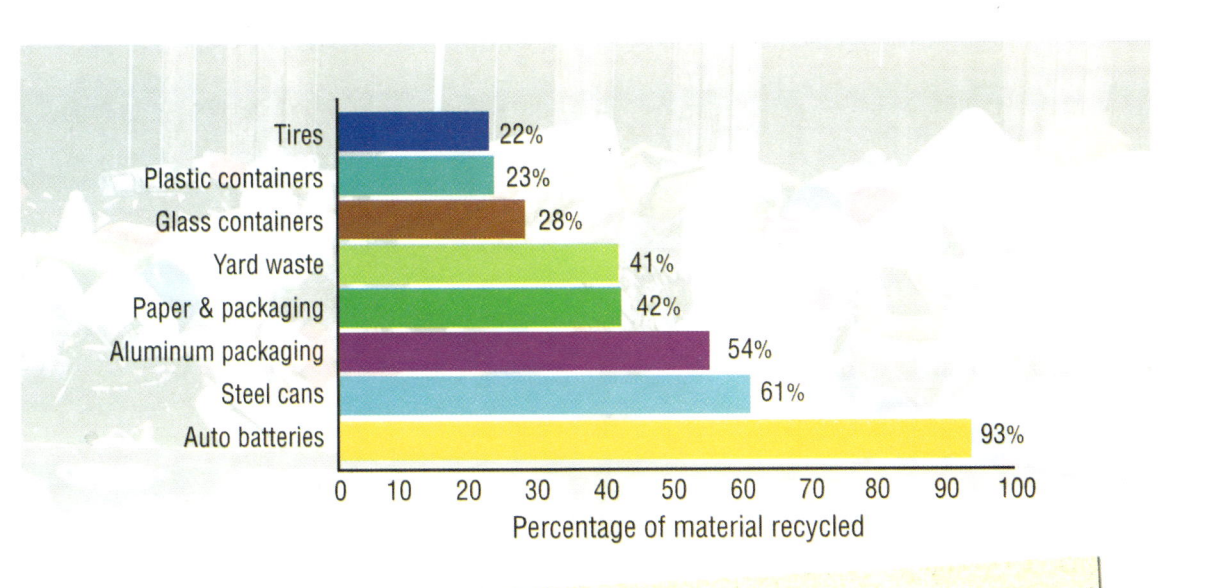

Material	Percentage of material recycled
Tires	22%
Plastic containers	23%
Glass containers	28%
Yard waste	41%
Paper & packaging	42%
Aluminum packaging	54%
Steel cans	61%
Auto batteries	93%

Activity

Making a recycled paper pad

Collect used paper that only has writing on one side. Place the paper together with the blank side up. Decide what size you would like your scratch pad to be. It can be the standard 8 ½" × 11" size, or you can cut the pieces if you would like a smaller pad. Find a piece of cardboard the same size as the paper, or cut it down to size. Place the cardboard in back of your paper stack. Staple the whole thing together. Use it as a place to take notes, make lists, or record things to do.

Conclusion

Think about all of the energy you use in one day. With the amount of energy that is consumed on a yearly, or even a daily, basis, it is no surprise that we are in danger of running out of our most common energy sources. Luckily, scientists have figured out ways to get energy from things we will never run out of. Renewable energy is more affordable today than it was 25 years ago. If researchers keep working on developing more efficient energy and consumers try to limit the energy they use, hopefully the world won't have to face a major energy crisis in the near future.

Internet Connections and Related Readings

Energy Information Administration Kid's Page (http://eia.doe.gov/kids/index.html)

Energy Ant guides you through this site, which offers a wealth of information about renewable and nonrenewable energy. Learn about coal, oil, solar energy, wind power, biomass energy, and more. The Kids' Corner provides links to information such as Energy News and Energy Pioneers. Learn about milestones in the history of energy and fun facts about energy. Go on energy field trips with Energy Ant. See photos of where he's been, and learn about different museums and interesting energy-related places. When you've navigated through the site, take an Energy Quiz to test your knowledge.

Energy Quest (www.energyquest.ca/gov)

This site is easy to get around and offers a fun format. Gather information about energy by clicking on Energy Story. In the Energy Almanac, find games and projects related to energy, such as comparing 1740 to today. Read an online energy adventure. Click on a timeline in the Energy Time Machine and learn about historical energy events. Find out about alternative fuels for vehicles, such as ethanol and hydrogen fuel cells, in the Transportation link. If you're in the mood for some fun, check out the Puzzles and Games link, where you will find energy coloring books, jokes and puns, and energy cryptograms. You can even enter a calendar art contest and ask Professor Quester for help with your homework!

Planet Energy (http://www.dti.gov.uk/renewable/ed_pack/)
On Planet Energy, you can enter the Renewable Energy Trail. Explore every path to learn all the secrets of renewable energy. To do this, you will first read the Energy Lord's introduction. As you travel the trail, you will answer questions. If you follow the trail to the end, you will receive a certificate proclaiming you an expert in renewable energy. After your journey, relax with some games, such as a memory game or renewable energy crossword.

Electricity by Darlene Lauw & Lim Cheng Puay. Presents activities that demonstrate how electricity works in our everyday lives. History boxes feature the scientists who made significant discoveries in the field of electricity. Science Alive! Crabtree Publishing, 2002. [RL 4.2, IL 2–5] (3396801 PB)

Heat by Darlene Lauw & Lim Cheng Puay. Simple text and experiments describe and demonstrate the principles of heat and how heat energy is produced. Science Alive! Crabtree Publishing, 2002. [RL 3.5, IL 2–5] (3396501 PB)

Nuclear Disaster at Chernobyl by Robin Cruise. The nightmare explosion and fire at the Chernobyl Nuclear Power Plant were just the beginning of the problems in the small Ukranian town of Pripyat. Its residents are still getting ill from the radiation. Artesian Press, 1993. [RL 4, IL 7–10] (4597801 PB)

Oil Spills! The Perils of Petroleum by Jane Duden and Susan Walker. When the *Exxon Valdez* slammed onto rocky Bligh Reef, 11 million gallons of crude oil blackened the clean water of Prince William sound. How common are deadly oil spills and what can be done to prevent them? Cover-to-Cover Informational Book. Perfection Learning Corporation, 1999. [RL 4.1, IL 4–9] (5623402 CC 9425401 PB)

- RL = Reading Level
- IL = Interest Level

Perfection Learning's catalog numbers are included for your ordering convenience. PB indicates paperback. CC indicates Cover Craft. HB indicates hardback.

Glossary

atom (AD uhm) the smallest unit of an element that still has the properties of that element

biomass (BEYE oh mas) **energy** from wood, animal waste, and agricultural crops and waste (see separate entry)

chain reaction (chayn ree AK shuhn) a series of events following one after another, each of which causes the next one

core (kohr) the center of the Earth

crude oil (krood oyl) oil that is naturally found underground

crust (kruhst) the thin, outermost layer of the Earth

emissions (ee MISH uhnz) harmful or impure substances, including greenhouse gases, given off by vehicles and factories

energy (EN ur jee) the ability to do work

energy crisis (EN ur jee KREYE suhs) a situation in which there are not enough sources of **energy** to meet demand (see separate entry)

extract (eks TRAKT) to get something from a source, usually by separating it out from other material

fission (FISH uhn) the splitting of an **atom** (see separate entry)

geothermal energy (jee oh THURM uhl EN ur jee) **energy** produced from the Earth's heat (see separate entry)

geothermal reservoir (jee oh THURM uhl REZ uhr vohr) a natural collection of hot water trapped underground in cracks or porous rock

greenhouse effect (GREEN hows uh FEKT) the heating of the atmosphere caused by greenhouse gases, including carbon dioxide

hydropower (HEYE dro pow ur) **energy** produced from water (see separate entry)

kinetic energy (ki NET ik EN ur jee) **energy** associated with motion (see separate entry)

46

magma (MAG muh) hot liquid rock beneath the Earth's surface

mantle (MAN tuhl) the part of the Earth that lies between the **crust** and the **core** (see separate entries)

nonrenewable energy (non ree NOO uh buhl EN ur jee) **energy** that is limited, or can be used up (see separate entry)

ozone (OH zohn) a greenhouse gas that is helpful high in the atmosphere but is a pollutant on the ground

peat (peet) deposits of dead plants in the bottoms of swamps that build up over thousands of years

petroleum (puh TROH lee uhm) **crude oil** and other products associated with it, such as natural gas (see separate entry)

plutonium (ploo TOH nee uhm) a highly toxic **radioactive** element (see separate entry)

potential energy (puh TEN shuhl EN ur jee) **energy** that an object has because of its position (see separate entry)

radioactive (ray dee oh AK tiv) used to describe a substance such as **uranium** whose atoms release a large amount of energy (see separate entry)

refinery (re FEYEN ur ee) an industrial site where **crude oil** is processed (see separate entry)

renewable energy (re NOO uh buhl EN ur jee) **energy** that is unlimited, or can't be used up (see separate entry)

solar energy (SOH lur EN ur jee) **energy** produced from the Sun (see separate entry)

toxic (TAHK sik) poisonous

turbine (TUR beyen) a fanlike structure that turns a generator to produce electricity

uranium (yur AY nee uhm) a **radioactive** element used as fuel in nuclear reactions (see separate entry)

wind power (wind POW ur) **energy** produced from the force of the wind (see separate entry)

wind turbine (wind TUR beyen) a device with a set of revolving blades used to create **energy** from wind (see separate entry)

Index

Bath, England, 31
biomass, 33–35
    ethanol, 34
Cape Cod Wind Association, 27
carbon dioxide, 34–35
Chernobyl Nuclear Plant, 17
coal, 7–9
Columbia Gorge, 26
Columbia River, 28, 31
crude oil (petroleum), 6, 8, 9–13
    extraction, 10
    history of, 9–10
    products, 9, 10
    supply, 12–13
Einstein, Albert, 14
energy
    crisis, 6
    definition of, 4
    kinetic, 5
    nonrenewable, 7, 14
    potential, 5
    renewable, 13, 21, 28
Exxon Valdez, 11
fluorescent lightbulbs, 38–39
geothermal energy, 31–32
greenhouse effect, 12
hybrid engines, 36–37
hydrogen, 35–36
hydropower, 28–31
layers of Earth, 31
Livermore-Pleasanton Fire Department, 39

Machu Picchu, 22
Mojave Desert, 24
Niagara Falls, 28
Nile River, 30
Nixon, Richard, 20
nuclear energy, 14–17, 20
    accidents, 17
nuclear waste
    plutonium, 18–19
    recycling, 19
    storing, 18–19
oil spills, 11
ozone, 12
photovoltaics, 24–25
rechargeable batteries, 41
recycling, 42–43
salmon, 30
    fish ladders, 30
solar energy, 21–25
    active, 23
    passive, 22
Sun, 21–22
thyroid cancer, 18
uranium, 15, 19
Volta, Alessandro, 24
wind power, 25–27
    turbine, 25, 26, 27
Yellowstone National Park, 32
Yucca Mountain, 18